afterlives' leaves

avi sato

springwaterspress

© Spring Waters Press 2019

Avi Sato has asserted all rights under relevant legislation to be identified as the author of this work. This is a work of creative poetry. Ideas are the product of the author's imagination and any resemblance to reality entirely coincidental.

No part of this publication may be reproduced or transmitted in any form or by any means without permission in writing from the publisher.

Poems.

Print ISBN 978-0-9877194-6-1
Digital ISBN 978-0-9877194-7-8

Issued simultaneously in print and electronic formats.

Published in Canada.

for you

who stood by me

when i forgot how to stand

of you

you speak of silence

simply sit and do not think

peacefulness appears

newer dreams than yours

dominate unthinking ones

fall not back to sleep

walking by dark streams

you are lost in their whispers

lose not your footing

introspection shields

your feet from paths of brightness

wherein you find the truth

no freedom comes

when you cry to the heavens

and cover your face

you within my mind

embody beauties unbounded

yet you do not exist

your tomorrows disappear

beneath horizons expectations

unclear in their silence

within created worlds

you replicate your escapes

only to return

i taste in your lies

a safety i found not once

when speaking the truth

your face forgets to smile

when eyes give in to twinkling

out of purest joy

awaken your eyes

behind consequential hats

imperceptibly worn

the touch of your hand

reminds it once was not there

you had not been born

a fragment of song

reflects reflects the darkest era

of a time before you

depressed keys

touch no great mysteries

with your songs

behind your veiled gaze

i stand ignorant in wonder

at who truly wears the cloth

between your verses

whitespace whispers negatives

louder than the words

dawn's hidden moisture

drinks from beneath your gaze

a soul aflame

your face shines upon

the majesty of evolution

while god plays with dice

your brutality

consumes my every moment

yet you are unaware

reflect on the grass

that bends beneath your footsteps

yet shall outlive you

morality dies

the death of a savior

when sin gives you pleasure

new idolatry

is masked by your freedom

to choose your idols

beyond your vision

you dance as a freed puppet

and see not the strings

tomorrow is free

of necessary actions

yet your thought remain

you speak of yourself

living within your choices

you change your clothes

the colors of dawn

pale before the field's reflection

the sound of a bell

action overwhelms

thoughts that you actively murder

as they give you doubt

contemplation reflects

happiness' long-drowned knowledge

you create this world

within the guidelines

of your sunswept gaze on my face

i see little else

i hear the flutes of your voice

echoing into the darkness

to call me to you

speak yet speak some more

taste in me a memory

of your lost lyrics

your mind a mountain

stands before my clouded sight

lighten my footsteps

your shadow before me

stands brighter than myself

where i lost my light

you taste the night

sweetness tinged with memories

of crimson sunsets

a single droplet

captures this moment in its

tranquil impermanence

i live only in your eyes

as you taste my energy

taste yourself in now

as one whose lips speak the truth

as afterlives' streams

of past

believe in a past

created in your image

remember not me

a history dies

within fires of ecstasy

yesterdays' phoenix

unwelcome mornings

shape yesterdays' memories

in their own image

remember me not
while i seek only absence
from the harshest gaze

surrounding the clock

is an aura of unknowing

describing today

cascades of memory

place rocks upon my pathway

may i lift my eyes

a book speaks volumes

of literal untruths

resting on my skin

no touch of past days

gives comfort of ages lost

behind morning mists

songs consume themselves

within unsilenced mourning

of artificial memories

call to the newly dead

to collect their own darkness

as you walk the river

of image

sit at tables low

resting on earth of new grass

look not at the skies

surfaces ripple

dragonfly descends quickly

reflections shatter

ancient white stone bridge

stands rebuilt over the path

prepared for its fall

nature's wordless songs

descend to the valley floor

answer in silence

frost inhabits wind

penetrating each footstep

lips sting from tea's warmth

incomplete images

shimmer in the distance

behind my eyes

negative spaces

taste of freedom to your soul

wherein you may end

caramel abounds

when the soul delights in warmth

against darker backgrounds

butterflies caress

palms awakened from numbness

awaiting dawn's gaze

ripples find my eyes

drawn toward unknowable fish

forgetting the crane

the stream caresses

footsteps outside my comfort

yet sand remains dry

create a new night

from the disappearing stars

to hold back the dawn

melodies arise

from sorrows' untapped cisterns

tasting of clean springs

the touch of new silk

petals alight behind eyes

sandals brush the sand

collapse offends me

tearing order from the world

in search of pleasure

no goodness comes from

those who focus on the self

they do not exist

of nature

trees shiver beyond sight

shadowed glances overwhelm moonlight

winds' embrace is dance

silvered echoes taste of silence

behind eyes once devoid of light

tomorrow only lives

in images of todays' ends

memories faded

the spirit breathes within all

who have no sense of belief

truth complete in innocence

knows no face beyond our end

yet we see new life

embodied in our every thought

alive in more than memories

a daydream

becomes as peaceful

as nightfall

dawn of new beginnings

shimmers just out of my reach

until yesterday

walking on moist pathways

feet propelled toward the stream

yet it is not distinct

behind the rain cloud

seasons of sunshine await

yet i feel them not

tomorrow brings the sun

drying rivers beside me

yet will i feel it

unthinking clouds

pass beyond my horizon

yet i think still

an overcast lake

reflects only mild darkness

beneath the hidden moon

butterflies mingle

beneath an oppressive haze

reflected in the stream

sunset alights here

separating wind from light

as day becomes naught

birdsong silences

itself beneath oppression's

nightly calls to prayer

a window on dawn

lights itself in the sunrise

prism to my morning

wind wanders in the distance

yet i feel it near at hand

unseemly in spring

a change from years past it comes

deep in its message

voice raised in abandonment

lost in destruction of hope

red dawn awakens

unconscious worlds of regret

to begin again

winds speak in silence

pressure changes in the air

taste of campfires

pouring sunlight's moisture

at trees' unpossessing feet

standing inattentive

petals fall before

branches' forgotten senses

standing amid wind

of life

circumspect beliefs

amass sanctuaries' lies

saying no more prayers

whisper joyful thoughts

into a silence that surrounds

the unspoken words

microscopes confound

heart as the place of liquids

where is now your love

spoken words

echo beyond my lips

no-one hears

harsh echoes

consume every hour

without sound

walk amid flowers

breathe deeply between petals' gaze

yet i say nothing

movement comes unbroken

to you who cannot resist

purchasing peace

tomorrow terrifies

with images of free choices

worked without a net

beneath the night's gaze

i cannot contain my fear

yet it follows me

into darkness' hours

i awaken as i sleep

amid terrors' depths

peace ungrasped yet free

shimmers beyond horizons

within my woken mind

within this moment

truth tastes itself onto eyes

dripping with the words

take pleasure in voice

broken onto rice paper

swallowed by your eyes

embody yourself

reflected in the heavens

before another

believe tomorrow

it is not simply today

endlessly repeated

newness arises

out of enlightenment's dawn

where suns may not set

call me by my name

create me in the darkness

speak within yourself

collapse offends me

tearing order from the world

in search of pleasure

no goodness comes from

those who focus on the self

they do not exist

dancing in my mind

feet stumble on pathways lost

to all but memories

flailing arms catch nothing

yet grip yesterday's losses

seeking salvation

i cannot be saved

from the terror that awaits

yet i must accept

truth falls upon me

weight beyond understanding

deflected by feathers

obsequious dreams

span darkness' limitless grasp

more real than morning

i pray in silence

begging not forgiveness

yet to forget this life

senseless abandon

shatters the night's welcome silence

losing the self

footsteps in darkness

echo terror in my mind

as i know them not

consuming my happiness

without the remorse of safety

unseen images

find themselves behind my eyes

without permission

yet in their presence i feel

alive in the pain they teach

collapsed gravestones

portray a life that is not mine

to judge yet i do

contemplating not the feelings

but actions driven by lust

flickering candles

wake me from meditation

oneness without light

i cannot illuminate

more than brief shadows of fear

songs consume themselves

within unsilenced mourning

of artificial memories

call to the newly dead

to collect their own darkness

as you walk the river

About the Author

Avi is a teacher and writer, one who desires to live outside the boundaries of a society lost to the artifice of equality trampled by misogyny, racism, and sexualized oppression, one who lives apart from the constructions of gender identity while crying for the necessity of that existence being apart from a world in fragments because of its unwillingness to shed its traditional attachment to manufactured roles.

They have lived and studied between Canada's east and west coasts, composing poetry on the shores of the Atlantic and pacific, holding dear within the heart the solitude that comes from standing at the edge of land with feet no longer willing to turn back toward humanity's lost humanity.

They are a proponent of art as an unrelenting walk along the pathway of beauty where ideas and thoughts and reality and existence take secondary role to language as a conduit for the simple pleasure of words living for their capacity to take the listener, the reader, even the writer to new worlds deep not in their knowledge but in their pure escape into beauty itself.

thought becomes my safety
yet i shiver against the cold
of tomorrow's randomness
taken to extremes
without beauty's touch

www.ingramcontent.com/pod-product-compliance
Lightning Source LLC
Chambersburg PA
CBHW031339060726

47590CB00007B/2539